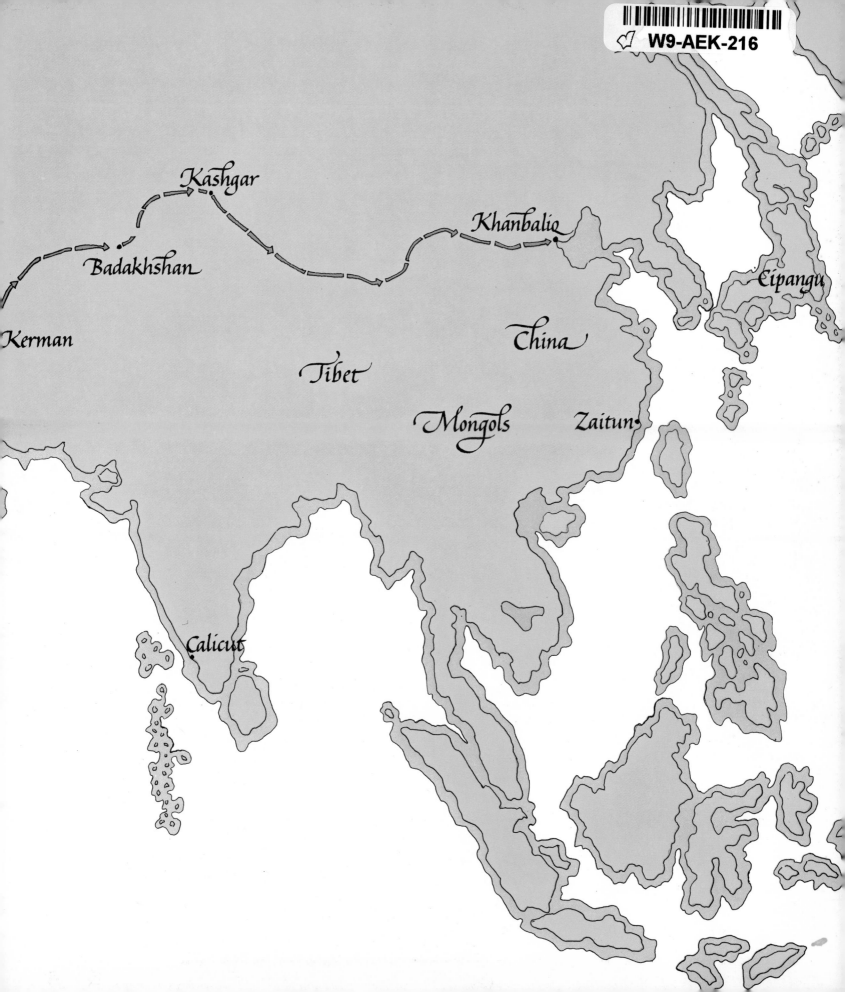

Kashgar

Khanbaliq

Badakhshan

Kerman

Cipangu

China

Tibet

Mongols

Zaitun

Calicut

Copyright © 1977 by Arnoldo Mondadori Editore S.p.A., Milano
English text copyright © 1982 by G.P. Putnam's Sons
All rights reserved. Published simultaneously in Canada by
General Publishing Co. Limited, Toronto.
Originally published in Italy by Arnoldo Mondadori Editore,
1977, under the title IL VIAGGIO DI MARCO POLO
Printed and bound in Italy by Officine Grafiche di
Arnoldo Mondadori Editore, Verona
First Impression

Library of Congress Cataloging in Publication Data
Ceserani, Gian Paolo.
Marco Polo.
Translation of: Il viaggio di Marco Polo.
Summary: Follows the adventures of the
thirteenth-century Venetian merchant who wrote
a famous account of his travels in Asia and his
life at the court of Kublai Khan.
1. Polo, Marco, 1254-1323?—Juvenile literature.
[1. Polo, Marco, 1254-1323? 2. Voyages and travels.
3. Asia—Description and travel. 4. Explorers]
I. Piero, Ventura, ill. II. Title.
G370.P9C4713 915'.042'0924 [92] 81-15685
ISBN 0-399-20843-7 AACR2

MARCO POLO

Gian Paolo Ceserani

illustrated by Piero Ventura

G. P. Putnam's Sons

New York

Venice–Home of Marco Polo

At the top of the boot-shaped country which is Italy there are two seaports that were once famous rivals. Genoa is on the left-hand side of the boot, sitting beside the sea. Venice, on the right-hand side, is built right on the water; its buildings springing up from islands connected to each other by bridges flung every which way. It is as if the city were rushing out to meet the ships coming into port. The streets themselves are winding canals which rise and fall with the tide and which are traveled by gondolas—long, flat-bottomed boats that curve up like a smile on either end.

In the thirteenth century Venice, called "the Queen of the Seas," was at the height of its powers. Its skyline rose in peaks and towers and swelled with the domes of churches. Its harbor was crammed with vessels coming in and going out. And right in the middle of this busy, prosperous century Marco Polo was born. He would travel farther than any ship in the harbor. He would become as famous as any Venetian ever born.

Merchants of Venice

Most of the people in Venice were engaged in the business of buying and selling, in trading, in shipping. The markets were filled with bales of silk from Damascus, sweet-smelling sandalwood from Timor, sacks of cloves and nutmegs, bags of cinnamon, rhubarb and myrrh from the East.

Like so many of the successful men in Venice, the men in the Polo family were also merchants. Indeed, when Marco was born, his father, Niccolo Polo, and his uncle, Maffeo Polo, were away on one of their frequent trips to Constantinople, the city where traders from the East met traders from the West. While they were away, trouble broke out between Genoa and Venice so that the sea was not safe to travel. The two brothers decided not to go home; instead they would go farther afield.

They went in the direction of the "Greek wind"—northeast. And they kept going for thousands of miles until at last they reached China, where the great Mongol conqueror, Kublai Khan, ruled.

Silks and Spices

So many luxuries that rich Europeans wanted came from China.

Spices, for instance. Not only did spices add flavor to food, but at a time when there was no refrigeration they helped to cover up the bad taste of food that had spoiled. Indeed, they were considered such a delicacy that sometimes they were served alone at the end of a banquet as a final treat. But, of course, spices were expensive. "As dear as pepper," people would say of anything that cost a lot.

Silk, too, originally came from China. Long ago the Chinese discovered that silk could be made from the thread that forms the cocoon of a certain worm living on the leaves of a mulberry tree. For several thousand

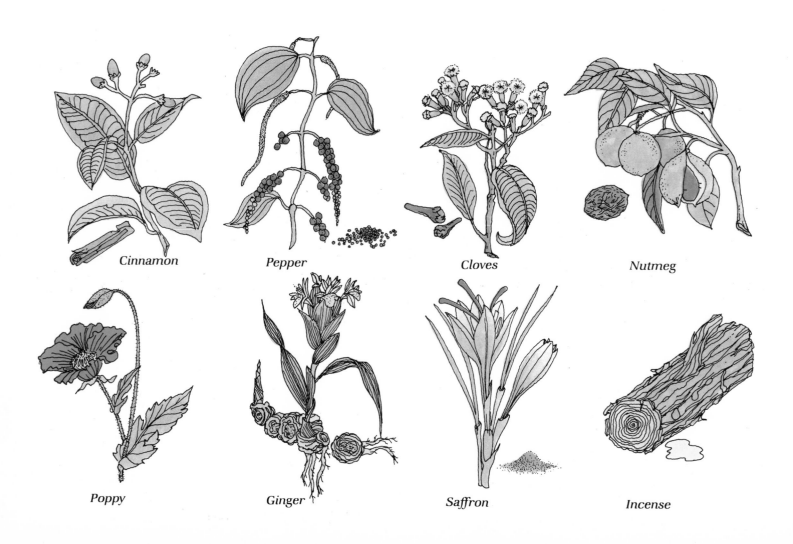

Cinnamon   *Pepper*   *Cloves*   *Nutmeg*

Poppy   *Ginger*   *Saffron*   *Incense*

years the Chinese managed to keep the process of making silk a secret, but gradually the secret leaked out to other eastern countries. Then in the year 550 (about 700 years before Marco Polo was born) two Persian monks hid the eggs of silkworms in a hollow reed and carried them to Constantinople. So with the help of these monks, Europe began to make silk too.

Not many Europeans ever got to China, but most agreed that a country that contained such treasures must be a mysterious and romantic place. What other wonders might it have?

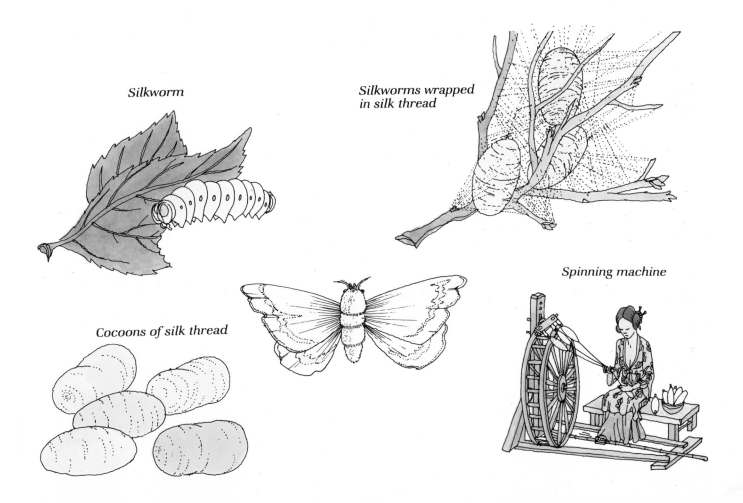

Silkworm

Silkworms wrapped in silk thread

Cocoons of silk thread

Spinning machine

The Great Adventure

As he grew up, young Marco Polo had no idea where his father and uncle were or if they were even alive. Marco was fifteen years old when Niccolo and Maffeo Polo arrived back in Venice. They had been all the way to China! they said. They had stayed at the court of the great Kublai Khan! What was more, they were going back. They had returned just so they could perform a favor for Kublai Khan.

This great ruler, it seemed, was not only wealthy and powerful, he was curious. He wanted to know how different people lived, what they knew and what they thought. So he had sent the Polo brothers with a letter to the Pope, asking for one hundred learned churchmen to come to China and teach what they knew. The trouble was that when the Polos arrived back in Europe, they discovered that the Pope had died. Back in Venice, they waited for a new Pope to be elected. They waited two years.

Marco was seventeen years old now and when his uncle and father were finally ready for their return trip, they invited Marco to go along. So on a bright summer day in 1271 Marco Polo said good-bye to Venice; he was starting out on his great adventure.

Of course the Polos called on the new Pope first. He gave them presents for Kublai Khan, but as it happened, he had only two friars, instead of one hundred, that he could spare. But the Polos took what they could get.

Then they all went to Laiazzo, a port in Armenia, the starting point for their journey.

Toward the Greek Wind

The Polo party had hardly started before they were caught in the middle of a war. Obviously traveling was more dangerous than the two friars had expected, so they turned right around and scurried home.

The Polos went on. They were bound for the city of Ormuz on the Persian Gulf where they could continue their journey by boat. But at Ormuz they couldn't find a single boat that didn't look as if it would fall apart in the first storm. So they decided to travel by land.

Back toward the Greek wind they went, passing from city to city. Some cities were built far up in the mountains where it was too cold even for birds to fly. Some cities lay at the edge of deserts in the path of blowing sand. Most cities hid themselves behind high walls.

The Great Gobi

The most dangerous part of the adventure was crossing the great Gobi desert. (*Gobi* is the Mongol word for desert.) It took thirty days to cross the vast sandy emptiness of the Gobi even where the desert was at its narrowest. Nothing grew in this endless sand, nothing lived on it, nothing even flew over it.

For a week the Polo party rested before starting across. They loaded their camels and horses with supplies of food and water. They tied bells around the necks of all their caravan animals so none would get lost. For the Polos knew that evil spirits of the Gobi were always on the lookout for stragglers, hoping to lure them away from their party, leading them to death. From the skies the evil spirits would call the lone traveler's name. They would beat on unseen drums. They would spread lovely liquid visions of water in the sandy wastes to tempt him farther away.

Fortunately, however, the Polo party managed to stay together and came through the ordeal of the Gobi without harm.

The Mongols

For some time, even before crossing the Gobi, the Polo party had been traveling through the land of the Mongols, the people who under Kublai Khan's grandfather, Genghis Khan, had conquered much of the world. These Mongols, however, did not seem much like Genghis Khan's warriors, famous for their expert horsemanship. Genghis Khan's horses, trained to make short, sudden turnabouts at full gallop, had led the Mongols in many victories. For just as their army seemed to be running away, all at once there they were back again, turned about and plunging into a new attack.

The Mongols that Marco Polo saw were shepherds who wandered over the countryside, setting up their round, felt-covered tents wherever they found grass

for their animals. As for their own diet, the Mongols disdained any kind of vegetable. Grass was for animals, they said, and animals were for men. They didn't care what animals. They would eat even cats, dogs or rats—if they were low on larger animals. They ate with their fingers, then wiped their greasy hands on their footgear to keep the leather soft.

But when they traveled, the Mongols didn't waste time carting meat around. They prepared dried milk by skimming off the creamy part and letting the sun dry the rest into a paste. Every morning each man put one-half pound of the paste into his leather bottle and added water. By mealtime the mixture, bouncing up and down on the back of a horse, had turned into a thin porridge, ready to eat.

The Great Buddha

Like Kublai Khan, Marco Polo was curious about the customs and beliefs of people. From time to time in his travels he met Buddhists, people who followed the teachings of Buddha, a saintly man born in India five hundred years before Christ. Often Marco visited Buddhist temples where people burned incense and worshipped before large statues of Buddha. Indeed, so impressed was Marco with the compassion of this religion, he remarked that if "he [Buddha] had been a Christian, he would have been a great saint with the Lord Jesus Christ."

Kublai Khan, who was interested in all religions, but never did get the one hundred Christians that he'd wanted, later became a Buddhist.

The Palaces of Kublai Khan

Marco Polo's journey was not only long, it was slow. In winter the party was often held up for months at a time. Once Marco took sick and the travelers stayed in one city for a whole year while he recuperated. They had been away from home for over three and one-half years before they finally reached the land of Kublai Khan.

It was summer when they arrived. Kublai Khan was in Shangtu at his summer palace. Ascending the marble steps, the Polo party was greeted by buglers, by soldiers, by noblemen dressed in their ceremonial robes. Kublai was delighted to see Niccolo and Maffeo again.

"But who is this young man?" he asked, pointing to Marco.

Niccolo bowed low. "Sir, this is my son who will serve you well."

Marco was impressed by the lavishness of the palace. Indeed, there seemed to be nothing that the Great Khan could want that he did not have. He even kept a company of astrologers on the rooftop to chant magic words for keeping storm clouds away.

In the fall the court (and the Polos) moved to the capital city of Khanbaliq (now Peking). The city was laid out in squares like a chessboard, with twelve gates, and three sets of walls, one behind the other. In the center stood the palace, more splendid than anything Marco could ever have imagined. In and out of the palace passed a constant procession of soldiers, bodyguards, noblemen, servants, all eager to wait on the Khan. Indeed, whenever Kublai Khan took a drink, everyone in his presence kneeled and a band played until he set his glass down again.

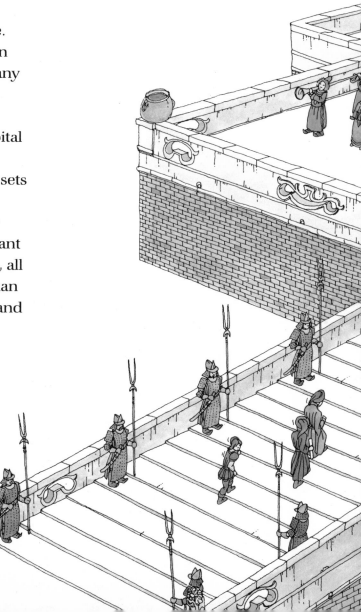

Green Mount

One of Marco's favorite spots was Green Mount, a park that the Khan had built on the top
of a huge man-made hill. No matter how cold it was, this park was always green for it
was planted with every kind of evergreen tree that the people in the kingdom could find.
Elephants carried the trees up the steep hill where they were transplanted.

Not only did Kublai Khan like trees, he liked what astrologers said about men who
planted trees: They would live a long life.

A Great Friendship

The Mongols whom Marco Polo met in China were far different from any he'd seen or heard about before. The Mongols in China had learned much from the Chinese whose civilization was older and more advanced. And no one was more eager to learn than Kublai Khan himself. Indeed, Marco Polo (who by this time could speak the Mongol language) found that the Khan was always asking him questions. And since Marco was both curious and observant, the two became great friends.

When the Khan went hunting, he took Marco with him. And what grand occasions these were! Ten thousand men were assigned to watch for game, according to Marco, and when the game had been sighted, the animals were let loose. Leopards and lynxes were used to chase deer. Lions went after boars, bears and stags, while eagles swooped down and caught wolves in their talons.

Kublai Khan soon began sending Marco out on special missions and was pleased with how well he did. Indeed, the Khan said that Marco was the only one of his emissaries who ever gave him news on his return. The others just did what they'd been told to do and had nothing more to say.

Traveling in China

As huge as the country was, the Khan had made traveling as easy as possible for his emissaries. He had established stations every twenty-five or thirty miles on the main roads where his messengers could eat and rest and where they would find fresh horses to replace their tired ones. He provided Marco with a sedan chair, many coolies, and a procession of soldiers and workers. And wherever Marco went, it seemed, he found surprises.

Paper money, for instance. Europeans had never thought of making paper money, but here it was the common currency. "Flying money," the Chinese called it

(*fei ch'ien*). Printed on pieces of black, cloth-like paper, each bill was stamped with the emperor's red seal.

Coal was another surprise. "Coal," Marco wrote, "is a black stone dug out of the mountains. When it is lit, it keeps the flame much better than wood." The Chinese used fire not only for cooking and heating but for warming water for baths. Marco Polo, who came from a part of the world where people rarely took baths, was amazed that the Chinese took as many as three baths a week.

A Land of Inventions

China is a land famous for its inventions. Some inventions, like this cart with sails, may not have had widespread use or lasted long, but on the other hand, the first spectacles that Europeans wore came from China.

Long before a system of printing was developed in Europe, China had invented its own system. Chinese characters were cut into wooden blocks which were then

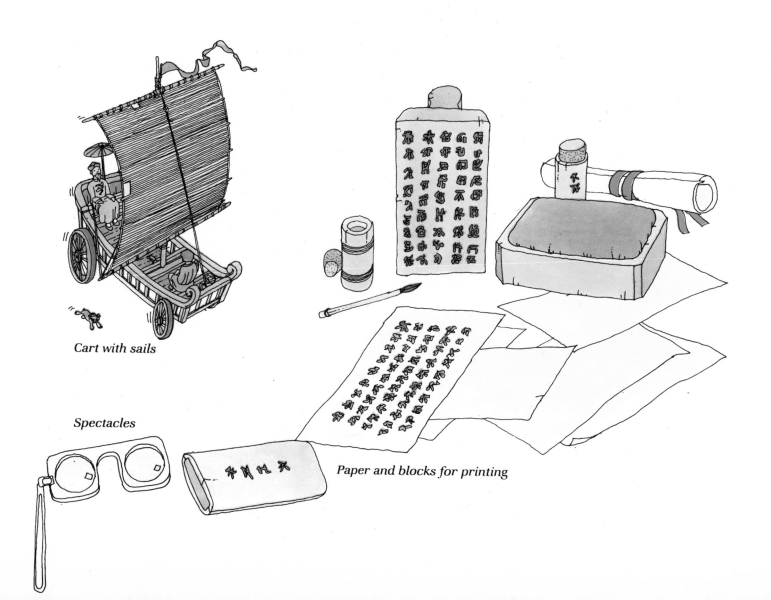

Cart with sails

Spectacles

Paper and blocks for printing

inked and transcribed onto paper. As many as 5,000 copies could be printed from one block.

The Chinese may have been the first to invent the compass. Certainly they were the first to develop firecrackers—not only the noisy kind but the flashy display kind as well.

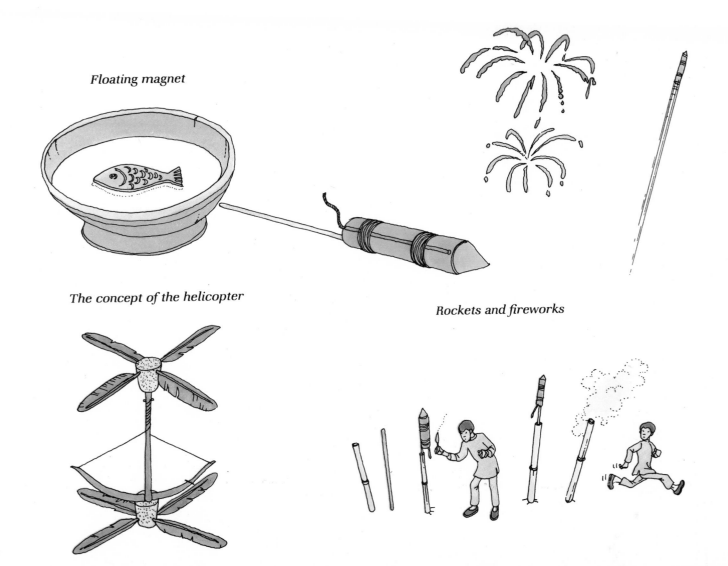

Floating magnet

The concept of the helicopter

Rockets and fireworks

Time to Leave China

Marco Polo, who was twenty-one years old when he arrived in China, stayed for seventeen years, until he was thirty-eight and the Khan had turned into a frail old man in his seventies. What would happen to the Polos, Marco wondered, when Kublai Khan died?

Marco had traveled long enough among the Chinese to know that many of them were unhappy with the Mongol government. Might they not go to war and try to take control of their country? Marco had seen enough of the Mongols to know that

they would certainly compete for power. He was also aware that he and his father and his uncle had enemies, people who were jealous of their friendship with the Khan.

All things considered, this seemed like a good time for the Polos to go back to Venice. So Niccolo Polo asked the Khan for permission to leave.

Kublai Khan said no. He liked the Polos too much, he said. He could not let them go.

Homeward Bound

As it happened, however, Kublai Khan was soon presented with a problem which, it seemed, no one but the Polos could solve. The Mongol wife of the Khan of Persia died, leaving instructions that her husband should marry someone of her own blood. Emissaries from Persia came to Kublai Khan who picked out a young Mongol princess for the Persian Khan. But before they could leave, war broke out in Central Asia and the emissaries were afraid to take the princess back by land. And since they didn't know the sea route, they were afraid to take her back by sea.

But Marco had recently returned from a special mission to India. He had traveled by water, so he and his father and his uncle volunteered to take the princess to Persia. Reluctantly Kublai Khan agreed.

So in 1292 the Polos set sail in a fleet of Chinese junks. Although the voyage was marked by one disaster after another, they managed to deliver the princess safely and in 1295 they arrived back in Venice.

At first the Polos had a hard time convincing their family and friends that they were really Marco, Niccolo and Maffeo back from China. And even when people were convinced, they had a hard time believing the stories that Marco told.

At the moment, however, no one had much time for listening. Genoa and Venice were at war. In 1296 Marco Polo, sailing in an armed merchant ship, was captured by the enemy and taken as a prisoner to Genoa where he remained for a year.

Meanwhile his friend, Kublai Khan, had died and just as Marco had predicted, the country was in a turmoil. (Thirty-five years later the Chinese succeeded in expelling the Mongols.)

"The Travels of Marco Polo"

People in Venice laughed at Marco's stories. "Master Millions," they called him, for he sprinkled his stories with such huge figures that no one could believe them. The Khan had a bodyguard of 12,000 horsemen! he said. He used 10,000 men just to carry his birds on a hunt! Every year on his birthday (September 28) he was given 100,000 white horses and so many other presents that it took 5,000 elephants and a train of camels to carry them all!

Marco thought that perhaps if his stories could be read in print, people would believe them. So while he was in prison, he dictated an account of his adventures to another prisoner, a specialist in writing. Marco didn't always describe places he had actually seen; sometimes he included accounts that he had only heard. Although he had never been to Japan, for instance, he depicted it in glowing detail.

When people read his book, *The Travels of Marco Polo*, some believed its stories and some did not. Christopher Columbus, who read the book more than one hundred years after Marco's death, believed every word—even the part about Japan. In a way, this was too bad because Marco had put Japan in the wrong place and that, of course, confused Columbus.

But people agree now that when Marco described what he'd seen firsthand, he was for the most part a good reporter, leaving the world with information it would not otherwise have had. But in his own day he was accused of outright lying. Indeed, as he lay on his deathbed (seventy years old now), he was asked to take back the parts of his book that were untrue.

Marco replied, "I have not written down half of those things which I saw."

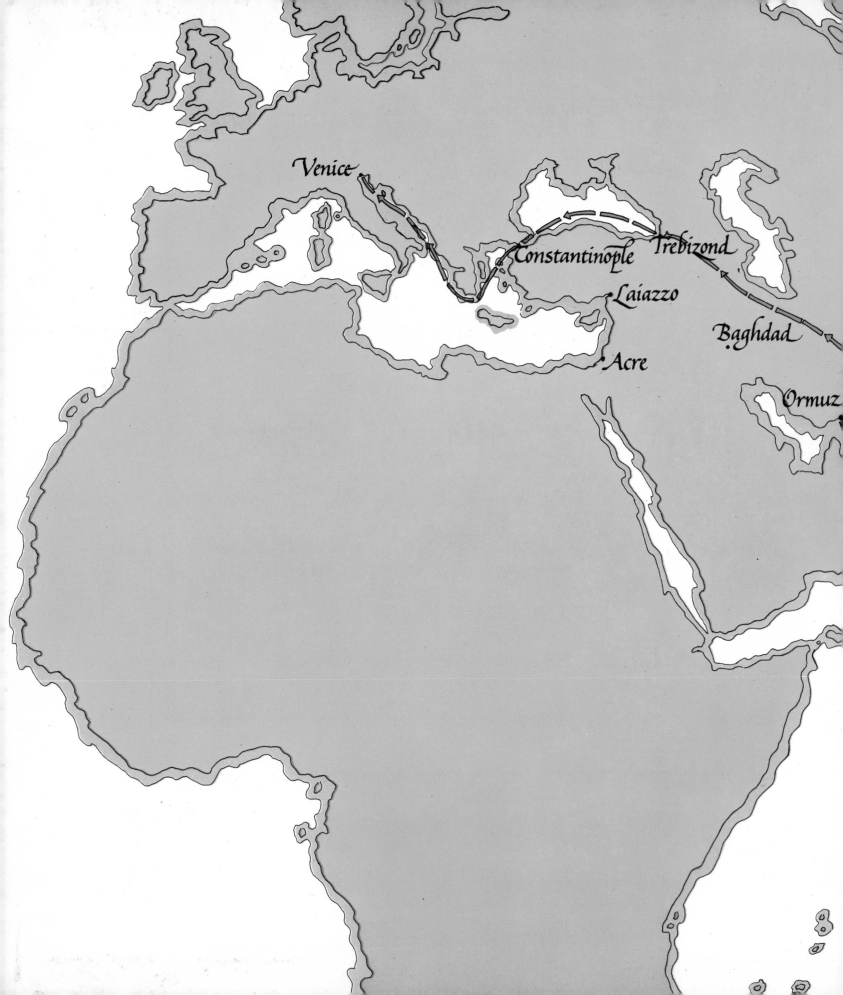

Venice

Constantinople

Trebizond

Laiazzo

Baghdad

Acre

Ormuz